IN CITO WE TRUST

SENSES OVER CENTS

2019 S

98 Sense

Collection of Poems

By Cito Blanko

Edited by Christina Santi

Published and Distributed by

"Cito Blanko LLC"

Bronx, NY [10466]

ISBN 13:9781080819911

Cito Blanko | 98 Sense

CONTENTS

How Much Does My Freedom Cost ?!

Introduction

I was raised and conditioned to see money as not only the gateway but a justifiable reason to do whatever I wanted. It was either you had enough money to take on the world, or none at all. For that reason, securing cash has become the focus for many, including myself. After spending 29 years on this earth, I realize that I've been lied to because whether I lost or gained money once that dopamine left my body, I felt the same: EMPTY!

The things that excited me in the past, no longer do. In retrospect, they probably never did. I was just addicted to a feeling of validation. I felt amazing when I bought sneakers in high school. But it was wearing them so my classmates could see that was the real value I wanted from the purchase. The social currency was what I was looking for, which included the respect and acceptance of my peers. I've had my heart broken with empty pockets and with money to spend, and either way, it felt the same in my soul. The things that changed were the resources I had to numb my pain.

> "I miss the drugs.
> I really miss the drugs.
> When I was high, even
> fake love still felt like a HUG."
> (49 cents)

If you did not need money, what would you do? Most people can't answer that question, because money has been the focus since we've been placed on this earth. How much does it cost? How much am I getting paid? SHOW ME THE MONEY! What happened to the value in knowing yourself, understanding nature, or making the world more aware of the war on our mind, body, and soul? I don't need money without knowledge. I value sense over cents.

Robert T. Kiyosaki, the author of *Rich Dad Poor Dad*, once said, "It's not how much money you make, but how much money you keep, how hard it works for you, and how many generations you keep it for." It is not about how much money you make; it's what you do with the money you have already. I've made several bad decisions with my money because my value system was based on vanity. I lacked self-confidence. Therefore, I needed things to make me feel loved. I did not know any better. The worst part is, I didn't want to be better because I was scared to grow. I was comfortable in my pain and trauma. Walking around with that much pain and resentment for the world wasn't healthy.

I've never stopped to wonder why I live this way or considered the elements that play a factor in my conditioning. I picked up habits on life's journey that helped me suppress the discomfort long enough for me to forget about it. But the truth is you never forget about it. Instead, you pack it away and hide.

"Being OK is a storage unit
for my sanity
because this world got me twisted
on who I was, who I am
and who I'm trying to be." (32 cents)

I knew I wasn't OK, but I never took the time or dared to understand what that felt like. I only had time for the present moment. As a young Black man in America, I wasn't awarded the luxury of thinking otherwise. I often question, I am a Black man first and a child of God second? I know who created human life, but who created race, and why did they intend for darker-skinned people to suffer the most?

There were days I hated the color of my skin. When you're young, you don't understand why the energy shifts once you walk in a room. Your parents can tell you stories of how the world will treat you, but it still won't prepare you for the anxiety waiting to squeeze your bones.

I struggle with society's ill-treatment of my people but its fascination with everything we do. How long do we have to wait for equality? But every day I walk this earth, I realize it's not going to happen magically. We must take it.

"So I'll wade in the water for my
day but, stop stealing our wave.
Our culture is copyrighted now and trust
me that LLC is on the way." (30 cents)

3 Cents

I'm tired of living on my colonizers land feeling mentally and physically enslaved. When I speak about oppression, I'm not doing it from a place of hate, but rather from a place of intrigue. How did it get this bad?

> "Someone told me Africa
> is where it all started.
> But who's fault is it that
> I'm wearing an American flag
> to school to represent
> my roots." (91 Cents)

People have lost the balance between the soul and the flesh. That's why this world is in mayhem. I forget who I am sometimes. But I don't stop living I keep trying new things and gaining experiences until I find myself again. I'm not going to apologize for my blessings when you laugh at my sins. I love to learn and mistakes are a part of learning. I don't like to call them mistakes anymore because even shortcomings are lessons. The enlightenment process isn't heralded because it only rewards the results and antagonizes the journey.

Through the process of growth, you learn more about yourself and your purpose. Discovering your dream is the most valuable thing this life can give you. I believe we are all here for a reason. Once you find your purpose, life becomes beautiful. You no longer rely solely on hope because you believe in yourself enough to set a goal and develop a plan.

"Dreams are fairy tales that lie to the truth. Find your purpose on earth and God will make a dream out of you." (18 cents)

Our ancestors have made sacrifices for you to live today, and you shouldn't take that for granted. I used to listen to everyone's two cents on what they thought my life should be. It was easier to listen to other people's point of view than to create my own plan. That is the inspiration behind the title, *98 Sense*. Even after you listen to the unsolicited two cents, you're left with your own 98 cents. The question is, which one are you betting on?

It can be hard to map out your life. It takes discipline to conceptualize the future without losing yourself in the present. It's necessary to write down goals and find stability in your uncertainty. If you don't, you'll wake up every day in the rat race, only dreaming about a life that can be achieved.

Sense over cents is the key to life! That doesn't mean you should do it for free. Value the purpose and the wealth will come. Value yourself spend time on learning yourself. Find your truth and always remember 98 sense is greater than two.

5 Cents

Who Am I Now?

"Who am I now?"
Is the story of my life
Throwback Thursdays
only shows the glory
but I want to read the
unedited version
of the story.
Everything I have now
is just a reflection of my past
So why, when something
goes wrong,
I blame me last?
I was late to work
the same way
I was late for class.
Somethings changed
but my bad habits
are still the reason I crash.

Note to Self

You think you know it all,
You think you have all the answers!
But then you realize
not having the answers
isn't the problem.
Finding out the purpose of the question
is what keeps me up at night.
My whole life I always had to find
an answer to solve the problem.
But who created the problem?
And why is a problem classified
as a problem?
I'm trapped in my mind
but sometimes
I forget I have the key.
I won't have an answer
to a question or a problem
because I don't accept that
society created this test.

How is there an answer to love?
How is there an answer to hate?
But we have an answer to beauty.

I have never seen an ugly flower
or ugly grass because ugly doesn't exist!
The beauty that surrounds me,
I can't see it because ignorance is bliss.

I lose the butterflies in my stomach
when I see these Instagram models.
I wish I only saw beauty from my eyes
but, society got me hypnotized on fake thighs!

What's the answer to life?
I hope I get it right
because we all live twice. Right?!
There are no answers to life
so there are no problems in life.
We create this fake test
and get mad
when we don't get
the answers right.
There's no right and wrong;
there's only love and hate.

My soul is trapped in my body.
My sanity is trapped in my mind.
My love is trapped in my heart.
My life is trapped in time.
So, if I can solve this, I'll be fine.

I'M A MAN

I spent the first 18 years
of my life waiting to be "The Man."
I've been trying to execute this plan
that shows the world that I know
how to stand on my own two feet.
But paying bills isn't better than playing 2K.
Manhunt was more fun than
being on the phone with Sallie Mae.
Waited my whole life to be a Man!
And now that I'm here,
I don't know where to stand.
Do I fight for the right to own land?
Or
Do I just cut dimes and throw bands?
Do I trade my future so I can sit in 1st class?
Or
Do I thank God it's Friday & troll?
on Facebook as my time past?
It was explained to me that,
you got real Niggas
And you got fake Niggas.
But what's the definition of "REAL?"
When I'm so high
that I don't know how life feels.
Waking up from a nightmare like damn
I'm in a nightmare still!
So you put down the condom because
her kingdom is the only place that feels real.
I'm tired of validating my manhood
with sex and checks.
Taking shots so that I can be happy for an hour but
I'm still in debt.
I walk these streets looking for a heart that beats.
but I guess not enough roses

---

made it out of the concrete.
I'm a Man, and I don't know
How much that means to you.
I want a family one day but,
can I love my wife for her truth,
and not because she waters my roots?
Can I be a father to the youth?
Can I be everything I wish my father was
and wasn't at the same time?
Can I hold back the pain of the world when I give
my future daughter a hug when she cries?
I don't know what being "A Man" means anymore.
But I realize that life isn't about keeping the score.
It's about making sure that
I have the right team on the court.

I know!

Dear
Every person
that went Celibate
to Save their souls.
        I know!

                        Dear
              every person that tried
                to keep their sanity
                    while trying to
                acquire their goals.
                        I know!

Adult Problems Cost Money

I forgot to pay my car insurance
and I kept my plates,
wrong mistake.
Now I have to wait 30 days
to put my foot on the break.
Well, at least they didn't tow my car.
I remember when that happened on a date,
Man!
That girl was going to shift her P into gear on my D
But there was no F—ing after losing my whip.
Wish someone made me download
the PDF manual
on all the mistakes
that was going to cause this shit.
What happened to valuing, "I'm sorry"
or "It won't happen again"?
I learned that sorry lost all its value after I set
the Guinness world record for over drafting!
I had to chase
Chase to get my money back.
Fun facts: Banks only give you
Two overdrafts back.
It took me three long years to learn that!
Adult problems cost money.
This isn't funny!
You ever lose an unlimited MetroCard
a day after buying it?
That will make you wish you were back in
Kindergarten and taking a nap
was the only requirement!
I remember when I use to spend $1.50 a day on food.
Now I spend half of my paycheck in Whole Foods
so that I can have enough energy to go to work
to make money and spend it on food.

Honey Buns, Nutties, and Doritos cost $1.50.
Now I have to pay 50 dollars
every time I glaze my honey in
her bun without the wrapper.
I pray for the day that toll booths go away.
We give the MTA half the tax to stay on track
and off our backs.
This is the end of my poem
because I don't have any more money for data.
I'm not broke,
I have to buy that MetroCard back
all the toll I've paid
the MTA should let me in free for a month
and month after that
This is officially the end of my poem
Can someone give me
some money to go home.

Cash app $citoblanko

1 CENT

Change doesn't only come
when you spend cash.
Change happens when
You make the
commitment
that your
future is going to
be better than your past.

Dreams

I have goals.
I don't have time to sleep
and acquire this fantasy.
I made a plan to
flee from everything I don't want to be,
because I refuse to be in the lost and
found of the world's sympathy.
I can see it in their eyes
when I tell them that I'm going to be free.
Either you spread your wings, or you lie in your sorrow
thinking about all the things you said you were going to do
tomorrow.
Why do we waste
so much time on fear?
They brainwash you to think that
8 hours of sleep is proper care.
That's the lie they tell you,
so you keep saying life isn't fair.
Life isn't sweet, but it's not bitter either.
Your body is just
Real Estate for the soul,
once you realize that you
can never get old.
But why do we spend
more money on gold
then we do
on our goals?
Look to the sky
when you're at an
all-time low.
Look for faith in places.
that have bones.
And wish for seeds,
but don't water to let it grow.

I have dreams,
I have goals, and I love to sleep
but, it's related to death so
I'd rather meditate while my brain
is manifesting a check,
so I can help build
a community center
to teach the youth
how to stay out of debt
and how going to
school for tech
is their best bet.
Dreams are fairy tales
that lie to the truth.
Find your purpose
on earth and God
will make a dream
out of you.
Be intentional with
your gift and be careful with your mercy.
The best lessons
I've learned in life are from the people that hurt me.
Keep sleeping if you want.
You're going to spend your whole life using 14
when your teacher asked for 12 size font.
Make sure you double space save some room for the mistakes.
And try to hand it in before it's too late.
Dreams can last forever, but goals have a date.

Shadows

It took me 29 years
to understand
why sons shouldn't
live in their fathers' shadows.
You'll find your own
darkness in due time.
I said I could never do
what my dad did
until I did it
a couple of times.
Never judge someone's pain
unless you've bowled in their lane.
I wish life
had instant replay
so I can learn
from all my mistakes.
I would change a few things
if I knew what
was at stake.
But those lessons
taught me
how to clean a
dirty plate.

No Mirrors

Reflection is the lesson life
left in the safe.
Some messages are meant
to be learned late.
Mirrors tell a story that
a selfie can't paint.
A picture is worth
a thousand words
but how are those
words heard?
Money is
a reflection of value.
Love is
the reflection of sacrifice.
And you
are a reflection of you.
Mirrors aren't only to see
if you're cute.
The purpose is for you
to see who I am?
While the seasons change
in this world that brings you pain.

I've Seen the Light

Greatness is only appreciated
when it's under the lights,
but I started
this movie at midnight!
I'm a zombie in this world
of fake trust
and made up lust
that's more valuable
than giving an f**k.
Watch me fall.
Watch me stand! Be scared of
this Black Man with a plan.
I am King! That's never
been to his land! Give me Hope!
Give me Truth! Don't give
me your love unless
it's bulletproof.
I've seen the light
but I still live in the dark.
My back is to the future
so I can learn from my past!
My Truth is in my roots
but the picture gets
blurry every time
I look for you.
I look up to find the answers
and then you whisper
to me: "Don't look that far."
But how am I supposed to be righteous
if my demons and my blessing wear the same scars?

THE NORTH STAR

Black women are not angry.
They had to develop
certain survival traits
because each generation
got a lot of practice
dealing with this world's hate.
You see her,
meet her,
feel her,
then leave her.
You refuse to see her beauty,
meet her soul,
feel her emotions,
so you leave her alone.
Beauty is in the eye
of the beholder.
I spent so much time trying to be Hova
that I didn't
see the dirt I was
leaving on my
Black women's shoulder.
I learned to understand
my Black women's pain
because sometimes she
has to play every
role in the game.
It's easy to call her angry
if you don't understand her pain.
Our women will always
be a reflection of our truth.
Let's stop exchanging pain
and saying all Black men and women
are the same and learn how to build trust
before we lust, so we can create a blueprint

that's tailor-made for us.
Black Women,
you are a Queen in my eyes.
No Women, No Cry
You're the strongest
part of our civilization
because you gave birth
to this nation.
If things are going to change,
it starts with how
we treat you.
You are the source of our roots.
Your body is the 1st place
that we discover our truth.
You're beautiful just the way you are.
You're the gateway to my freedom.
Thank you for being my North Star.

On the road

who am I to lie?
who am I to fly?!
who am I to die
in this empty
perception of life?!
I got on the road to redemption
& I looked both ways,
but I was surprised
when I found my old footprints
in this maze.
why complain about anything
when you have the power to
make a change?

Celebrating My Skin

Black women are so divine.
Beautiful, strong
and are so kind until
you cross that line.
Why must she fight for respect
that's just given to others?
Why must she pledge for Black men to love her?
I hate the perception that I help create.
No more chicken wings & fries, we need those dates.
So we can create a healthy environment
where we can sit down and relate.
I finally understand what's at stake.
This is bigger than Me. This is bigger than We.
Billions of people have walked this earth
Across different seas planting seeds to grow.
So each generation after it can know.
I'm not here to stunt my people's growth.
Don't tell me love doesn't have a color
while this world holds a paintbrush full of hate and
picks my color to exterminate.
I was a prisoner to your
system of mental oppression.
That filled my body with so much hate.
Now I'm celebrating my skin.
By choosing a soulmate that looks
like the woman, I was carried in.

Red & Blue Flashing Lights

Just because it's the law doesn't
mean that it applies to us.
So when the cops pull us over,
get ready,
because they're going to ask for
more than your registration and ID.
They're going to ask for your dignity because they
know they can cross that line without any fines or
getting convicted of any crimes.
I ain't pass the bar
& I know a little bit that sometimes the best thing
to do is have them search your whip.
Jay-Z got "99 problems"
and being rich ain't 1.
I know what tears look like
from a mother that lost her son.
I've had my heart drop when cops
unbuckled the strap on their gun.
I want to make it home so ain't no
"You can't do that officer" or
"I have my attorney on the phone."
"Yes, I can step out the vehicle."
And "No, I wasn't texting on my phone."
"I don't have alcohol
on my breath, and
no weapon is in the car."
Just the weight of the world
on my chest.
Thinking *why didn't I stay home*
or *why did I tint my windows?*
Why am I Black?!
But those thoughts stop once he opens
my trunk and looks for the strap.
He opens up my glove compartment

and asks, "What's that?"
I reply saying,
"It's whatever you want it to be,"
so I don't end up in
the back of your squad
car with wrist scars.
. I ask myself, *Would I have stopped me?*
Tinted windows, music blasting
and a car full of the crew.
If I was a cop, would I stop me too?
Like this ain't about the color of my skin.
He had a job to do ...
Right?
Every time I get in trouble with the law,
it can't be because of my race
he's just talking like that to me because
I didn't know my place.
It can't be because I'm Black.
These are questions that cross
my mind while I drive home
physically fine but, this trauma
will never leave my mind
but I'm happy that
I made it home this time.

Hangman

They played hangman
with our fathers,
Pulled the cherry stems
from our daughters.
Gave plea deals to our sons
without seeing lawyers.
Don't tell me racism isn't alive.
As long as there's a race,
Black people will
be fighting
for our place.

Puer[1] Black

I see that society doesn't
value me as a human being.
My humanity is just a
broken record of
the cruel methods you use
to tunnel my oppression.
You stole gluttony from Rome
and the land from the natives.
Being honest with you is a waste of time
because you don't understand father time.
Patience has never been a part of your grind.
America, you're a grape,
but you could have been wine.
You wrote the words of freedom
but never lived up to the lines.
We have the highest incarceration rate in the world
but we're not even in the top 10 in countries,
that do crimes.
The due process is lost in the cost, and
you kill my people so that you can get more
overtime from your boss.
Being Black in America
means that I'm a stock
and my sorrow
and my demise is what keeps me
on the block.
You trade my time from cell to cell
like I'm a disease.
white supremacist
You're the white blood cell inside of me

---

[1] Puer aeternus (sometimes shortened Puer), is Latin for "eternal boy." In mythology it is a child-god who is forever young. Puer is also a fashion brand by Noel Bronson.

I'm shattered glass that
got put back together with
different pieces. But I still live thru
Martin Luther's thesis
A dream is only
a dream when you're sleeping.
I'm woke, so I remember
Everything that I'm thinking.
I sign my last name & I think about
Every step I took on this earth
With a slave master's hand on my ink
I read and know my history.
Writing those letters still brings pain to me.
Land of liberty, home of the brave.
I never picked cotton, but I still have your name.
Don't judge me because I spend my little change
on diamonds and gold rings. Those are
natural resources you stole from my motherland.
This land is your land; it isn't mine.
White supremacy stands strong
from California to the New York Islands.
This land was made for you, and not for me.
You made that very clear when you changed the
Statue of Liberty. I guess it was too
embarrassing to have Black women stand in your company.
You are all about the cream[2]
but, we are the black coffee
that keeps you up while you were doing your thing.
So I'll wade in the water for my
day but, stop stealing our wave.
Our culture is copyrighted now and trust
me that LLC is on the way.

---

[2] Cream is also a slang term for money.

Are You OK?

Yea I'm fine... I think?
When you ask if I'm OK,
What do you mean?
Do I love money more than my dreams?
Do I feel empty when staring at Porn on screens?
Am I happy?
Do I even know what that means?
Being OK is a storage unit
for my sanity
because this world got me twisted
on who I was, who I am
and who I'm trying to be.
I haven't seen a meme
that describes that mood.
So asking me if I'm OK is kind of rude.
If you wanted to talk to me,
you would say,
"What's on your mind?"
But you asked me,
"Am I ok?"
So I reply
"I'm fine!"

Pray 4 Me

Nobody is praying 4 me!
The sad part is, I know that's a lie.
I want the praise from
the people with the deluxe apartment in the sky.
When am I going to get my peace of the pie?
3:14 am, and my subconscious is on a trip,
looking for some experiences that I regret.
My fear is holding on while my
insecurities are telling me never to let go.
What makes today so special?
Do I still have to pay full price for my dreams?!
There's a hole in my heart that
wants 15% off on love, please!
I tried to steal someone's mind,
but the sensor went off after
I crossed out the line
in the store-ry of time.
Twenty-four sentences with 60 words on each line.
Your pen is your actions, and your hand is time.
So what's your rhyme?!

MAMA

I can't imagine a world
without your love.
The days you made me
feel better with a hug.
A mother gives you more
than the gift of life.
They stay around to make
sure, you're doing it right.
And sometimes we may disagree
or fight but, once the dust settles
most of the time, you were right.
Twenty-four hours isn't
enough to express all of my love.
I want to repay you for all the times
you didn't think twice.
You gave me love sometimes
when I felt like I didn't deserve it.
I want to be a success, to prove
that all the things you did for me
were worth it.
I love you, mommy.

Is God Real?

Do you believe in god?
I know what it feels like to walk
in the dark.
But it's scarier to walk when
you're free.
You should hear how me and God fight.
I go the wrong way,
and he disciplines me
but not before I learn the lesson
he was trying to gift to me.
God is Real!
If you don't believe me then close
your eyes forever
and tell me how life feels!

Yo Cito

Your mom is looking for you!
I told her you were in a trap!
But you weren't flowing on a Metro beat.
You're lost in this social critique
By 28 I was supposed to have a Benz
and money long enough that
it doesn't matter
where me and my friends go.
Dubai or Turks & Caicos.
By this age, I was supposed to be swimming in the loot,
but my work ethic wasn't enough proof.
I never had dreams of shooting hoops or
rapping in a booth,
I just wanted the truth.
I felt like I was drafted in the 1st round
Then I got waived.
Getting a degree sometimes
feels like you're trying to make the NBA.
But graduation isn't like draft day;
they get a check while I get debt.
So now I'm back home
living check to check.
Working the same job as the kids you
said had no future and would get left behind.
At that time marijuana was
the only thing that I trust.
I was so high that I couldn't feel my face.
I felt like my soul was wrestling with fate.
Hugging my mother & feeling her warm soul.
Her hugs remind of the days she let me stay home
from school knowing that
I was faking my cold.
Eyes bloodshot red.
I know if I looked into

her eyes, it would
give me the clarity of the
man she wants me to be.
I know my mother
is looking for me.
Tell her
I'll soon come home
because I have to
clean my soul.
So the next time I give
her a hug my spirit isn't so cold.

Wake Up

Wake Up!

Why?

Wake up, bro!

1 more hour?!

Wake up.

I'm going to work on you.
tomorrow.

You said that
yesterday!

Well, I mean it today.

I'm not going to be
here forever.

Don't leave me like
the rest of them.

They didn't leave you.
You let them die.

Well if you leave
another dream will arrive.
Hello?
Yo!
Come Back.
I'm scared of you.

Well I hope you can deal with the regret
you keep acting like you know
how much time you have left.

FINISH YOUR BREAKFAST!

Everybody wants to eat but
I wonder
Who invented the fork?
How did they know that
four points can pick up pork?
Growing up, using your mind meant you were a dork
or too smart for sports.
Which never made sense to me.
But I couldn't see past the basketball court.
Everybody eats, is the expression,
But can I teach all of you a lesson?
Eating shouldn't be the goal,
you should learn how to cook
because that's the weapon.
Breakfast is the most important meal of the day
because it starts the inception.
Too many young minds out here
half-stepping the lessons
walking in this world with no direction.
It's called a mind-frame because
it's a mind game from the day you were born
you have to watch what makes your mind change!
You have a dollar mind, with a penny grind
because you only see life for the dollar signs.
Age 0-7 is the membrane.
That's when you didn't care if your friends changed.
You were trying to color while drinking cool-aid.
But you were exposed to
big chains and the drug game.
Seeing your pops get jumped
at 6 made you reframe!
They work so hard after the age of 7
to teach you the lessons of life
but they didn't get the message!

If you never finished the eggs on your plate.
Or wondered why Vegeta from
Dragon Ball Z hairline wasn't straight.
I understand why you eat so late.
Because you never valued a hot plate
that can only come from that love place.
I'm not talking about soul food or
how you traded the gospel
for chicken and waffles.
I'm telling you that you left your mind on the table,
looking for everything in
this world that can keep you stable.
The food from Breakfast can taste so reckless
when you eat it for lunch trying to fulfill the message!
Pancakes are the love
while the syrup is the trust.
Eggs are the plug
while bacon is the drug.
Cheese is the personality
because when it spoils, it shows your reality.
So many of us never finished our Breakfast,
searching for our 1st meal in this world that
will leave you breathless.
So eating what they give you
became your preference.
You only know a hungry life,
so teaching people how to eat is your only advice.
Hunger creates depression,
that's why crabs pull down their friend,
even though they know where they're heading.
A boiling pot seems like heaven
when you're walking in a world.
Going thru depression.
Breakfast time is over,
but it doesn't hurt to look
over your shoulder to

see the breakfast you left
cold while trying to be bold
in this world that drank its Folgers.
So I think it's time to start thinking
about the breakfast our kids
are going to dig in,
so they never feel hungry while thinking
about how to change the world we live in.

FINISH YOUR BREAKFAST!

Grapes in A MicroWave

What happens when you
put a grape into a microwave?
They say it explodes into little pieces
I don't know if that's a fact.
The grape might have been seedless
so it had no DNA.
It can't have loyalty or
royalty without a soul.
We traded its seeds in, so
It can hang its
neck on a gold chain
for
6 seconds on a vine.
If you waited a little longer,
you could have been a glass of wine.
We think that we can beat Father Time.
If Langston Hughes
is a raisin in the sun,
then I'm a grape
in a microwave
that's following
these micro-waves of trends
they created to keep us mentally enslaved.
My ancestors weren't only slaves.
They drew hieroglyphics in caves and could
tell if the river was going to overrun
based on the Sun's rays.
Now we struggle to
raise sons because we don't rise to the occasion.
to change the system that
values cents more than sense.
How is this life fun,
when raisins are still burning in the sun?
What does it mean to be free when pollution is

still poisoning our lungs?
They treat us bad because of some of us.
But the truth is they're scared of
the power of the sum of us.

School Lunch

The circle of life started
with school lunch pizza and
grabbing chocolate milk out the freezer.
Who would have known that lunch-tables
were the first place that classism would exist?
If you finish your breakfast, then you had
the option to choose
where you're going to eat n' piss.
Seats are chosen with care
because once you're an Outkast
the big boys overwhelm you with fear.
I used to be excited because
they had PB&J.
now I think about all the food for thought
I lost trying to be a boss.
Now the jokes on me,
My pay rate reflects what I don't know
Could have been in an office but
now I'm knocking on a front door.
Every day I feel another shovel covering my dreams with dirt.
I can hear my coach telling me to go to class.
He used to say, "These high school days fly by fast."
I was worried about cash & ass.
I used to feel like the sky was the limit.
Now I don't have time for breaks
because I have to make up for all my mistakes.

Save The Date

Greatness is never
understood in
the lifetime of its truth
so greatness
is only appreciated
after you leave
the booth.
So unbutton the blazer
and loosen up your tie.
Set inside of your truth
& greatness will come alive.
Save the date
that you told this world
that you were going to be great.
And don't get mad when
your applause comes late,
just do whatever it takes
to show this world that
you are one of the greats.

Never Fear

Fear is my best friend.
Nothing can bring me
closer to me than you.
You were the only
one there on my
first day of school.
The first football game,
and the 1st time shorty
gave me brain.
Fear is elite; it's the only thing
that can make me
better or worse
in a heartbeat.
You hate fear because
you treat fear like a stranger.
I love fear
because fear is my neighbor.
Fear is in every step of the way.
The only thing that
relates to your last breath,
that unknown date
When there's no more
time on your slate.
But the fear of death is what makes
my grind tick because I want to
do as much as possible before
I leave this ship.
So if fear is the only thing that keeps me on track,
then fear is the only one that has my back.
False Evidence Appearing Real
Red or The Blue pill?

The Process

When you reverse
engineer the game,
You understand why fame
can be your biggest shame.
Because people love you for your mistakes
and are happy to eat
any crumbs you've left on your plate.
You have to live to create!
experiences change perspectives while
hard work turns into blue-bills.
The dead Presidents were dead
b4 the register.
So why live your life for something
that can only change with a price.
For the love of money is the root of all evil.
We love it so much
that credit became the sequel
of our demise.
You're trying to walk
on water in a hurricane.
That's the analogy I use
to describe the game.
You love the finish line more than race.
I don't care about the icing
show me the cake.

No Pain, No Gain

I laugh at the days
I was scared to be me.
When I acted like the people, I saw on TV.
The days I spent not being
true to my soul, were the days
I felt so cold, so low,
and lost in this place.
I thought was my home
Every door I opened,
I felt more alone.
I looked in the mirror
Wondering if I was the clone
because this can't be me
This can't be you.
What happened to the passion
we had on the 1st day of school?
Do you remember the days
when being cool used to rule?
Now, all we do is get drinks and eat food.
Who are you?
Sometimes I think about
who I used to be
& the memories are scary.
Calling women hoes.
Making fun of people's clothes.
Stashing O's for my bro!
There's so much more.
Lord only knows,
I'm crying because my soul is exposed.
I hate tears because
they never tell the same story.
I cried because of fear.
I cried because I wish
my grandmother was here.

I cried because some days
I felt like
I shouldn't be here.
But I'm a ghost so
I'm only focused on my goals.
But having so much power
can be such a lonely road.
Especially when friends say
"I'm here."
Just because you're present
doesn't mean you have gifted
me your care.
I guess I'm not strong enough
to tell you how weak I am.
I don't have suicidal thoughts,
but I wonder what certain people
would say at my grave.
One of my deepest secrets is that
sometimes I feel like a lame when
I'm singing Jesus name.
I am a sinner, but that's old news.
I tried walking in my old shoes
, but they don't fit, and these
new kicks hurt a little bit.
I hate that
I need people to feel love.
I miss the drugs.
I really miss the drugs.
When I was high, even
fake love still felt like a HUG.
This is a hard world
to deal with when you're sober.
But playtime is over.
I've decided to live in my reality
because this is my destiny.
I don't run from the pain anymore.

I tried to smoke but
the high ain't the
same no more.
Drugs numb me from the pain.
But I realize the lessons
I needed to gain
was in my pain.
So now I accept life for what it is.
The only way to be the
People's champion is to take
THE ROCK off your chest.
And let you know that life is hard and
sometimes you still lose even when
you try your best.
But being better today than you
were yesterday is worth more than a check.
We all learned how to crawl before
we learned how to take a step.
So take it one day at a time, it's never too late!
Don't stare at the destination
because the ETA might scare you away.
Just stay true to the essence of your
soul and remember that 30 isn't old.
Just write down your goals!
You can keep them private;
the world doesn't have to know.
Just let it go, don't be *frozen* in this life.
I heard that song when
I was watching my niece and
it made me think twice.
Like maybe kids have the recipe to life.
Be bold!
Be spontaneous!
Be adventurous!
Be true!
Life changed when

I looked up the definition
of enough &
I saw a picture
of YOU.

ODE TO BASQUIAT

YOU WERE THE GENIUS CHILD
THAT I WISH NEVER GREW.
YOUR MESSAGE
BROKE ALL THE RULES.
YOU ARE AN ICON ON THE BRICK WALLS
OF SCHOOLS.
YOU WANTED TO BE KNOWN
BY THE CRUEL WACK PEOPLE
LOOKING AT WHITE WALLS
DRINKING WHITE WINE.
THEY NEVER UNDERSTOOD YOUR MIND.
THEY WORE WATCHES, BUT YOU
USED SAND TO DEFINE YOUR TIME.
I WISH YOU COULD SEE SoHo NOW.
IT WOULD TURN THAT FROWN UPSIDE DOWN.
YOU GREW UP IN A WORLD THAT
DIDN'T SEE YOU AND THEY COULDN'T UNDERSTAND YOUR CANVAS.
ART IS NOTHING WITHOUT PAIN.
MUSIC IS NOTHING WITH FAME.
SO LIFE IS EVERYTHING THAT WAS
IN YOUR TRUTH. YOU'RE THE RADIANT CHILD
FROM THE GREY BAND.
I WISH YOU WERE STILL AROUND
SO I COULD SHAKE YOUR HAND.
YOUR ART GAVE ME LIFE
SO IT'S ONLY RIGHT
THAT I SAY THAT YOUR
THE GENIUS CHILD THAT
CREATED THE WILD SO
YOUR SOUL CAN SMILE.
I KNOW IT TOOK A WHILE FOR
THE WORLD SEES YOUR CROWN.

MY THOUGHTS SPEAK

IF MY THOUGHTS COULD SPEAK,
IT WOULD SAY, I PRAY MY LORD
MY SOUL TO KEEP.
THIS SINFUL WORLD USED TO BE A GENTLE GIRL.
BUT NOW ALL I SEE IS A
PEN-CEL WORLD.
TOO MANY DAYS ON THE 2 TRAIN
THINKING ABOUT THE INSULIN
FLOWING IN MY MOMMY'S BLUE VEINS.
LACK OF OXYGEN TO THE WORLD'S BRAIN,
LEFT MOTHER EARTH'S MOUTH
WIDE OPEN IN THE RAIN.
HOW MANY DAYS REMAIN?
IS WHAT GIVES MY THOUGHTS SO MUCH PAIN.
WHEN I DIE, DO MY THOUGHTS
STAY THE SAME OR DO THEY DIE
WITH MY BODY FRAME?
TRAPPED IN THIS BODY GAME WHERE THE FOOD I EAT
AND KNOWLEDGE I SEEK
IS WHAT MAKES MY THOUGHTS SO DEEP!
BUT SOMETIMES YOU DON'T HEAR A PEEP
WHEN MY THOUGHTS
ARE ASLEEP IN PEACE.
THAT'S WHAT YOGA DOES FOR ME!
I WISH ADAM NEVER BIT THE APPLE
OFF THE TREE BUT THEN STEVE JOBS
WOULD HAVE NEVER MADE ME.
THE PHONE THAT I'M USING
TO TYPE THE THOUGHTS
MY BRAIN READS.
MY THOUGHTS COME WITH A FEE.
OVERTHINK & YOU CAN GET LOST IN THE SAUCE.
FORGET TO THINK, AND YOU'LL SPEND YOUR WHOLE LIFE WITH
A BOSS. SO MY ONLY QUESTION IS,
HOW MUCH DOES MY FREEDOM COST?!
THE REALITY IS, THE DAY OF
BEING FREE IS NEVER GOING TO HAPPEN

**BECAUSE MY MIND IS THE SLAVE AND
THE MASTER OF MY THOUGHTS!**

CIRCLES & LINES

SOCIETY INVENTED THE CORNER.
THINK ABOUT THE SHAPES IN A DIPLOMA.
THINK ABOUT THE DOPE, THE HUSTLE & THE GRIND,
SOCIETY INVENTED THE LINE
BECAUSE EVERYTHING THAT HAS CIRCLES IS FINE.
THINK ABOUT THE CURVES OF A DIME.
LET'S TALK ABOUT CIRCLES AND LINES.
NOTHING IN NATURE IS STRAIGHT
NOT TREES
NOT MOUNTAINS
OR LAKES.
BUT SOCIETY WANTS US TO BE FAKE
BECAUSE ONLY LINES CAN BE MULTIPLIED BY 2 OR 4,
DEPENDING ON THE CLONE OF THE MIND.
TIME IS A CONCEPT, AND MONEY IS A CRIME.
MONEY MAKES YOU LOSE THE VISION OF TIME
& KEEPS YOUR MIND IN 4 LINES.
X OR A CHECK IN A BOX
EQUALS DEBIT BUT
WE STILL BET OUR TIME ON MONEY
AND CALL IT THE GRIND.
THE ONLY HIS–STORY I KNOW
IS A STORY WITH A PERIOD ON A LINE
MY HISTORY WAS ILLUSTRATED THRU SIGNS
THAT ARE UNIQUE LIKE NILE RIVERS, CAVES & MINES
BUT WATERFALLS DON'T FALL IN YOUR MIND.
THE ONLY TIME
YOU CHECK THE TIME
IS WHEN LA & NEW YORK ILLUSTRATE
WHAT THEY FIND
BUT AS LONG AS WE KEEP THESE NIGGAS IN LINE.
THE SENTENCE CAN RUN! FOR DAYS WHILE RED MARKS
THE GRAMMAR OF THE NIGGAS
WHO DIDN'T LISTEN TO GRANDMA.
SO AFTER SENTENCE, THEY LET YOU
KNOW A CIRCLE IS ONLY
GOOD AFTER A LINE.

PERIOD.
A WATCH IS THE ONLY CIRCLE THAT MOVES LINES
THINK ABOUT EVERY CIRCLE WITH LINES
THE ONLY CIRCLES THAT DON'T
FIGHT LINES ARE IN THE SKY.
SUNS MOONS AND THE RADIUS OF MY TESTICLES
DROPPING ON EVERY LINE THAT TRIES TO DEFINE
THIS MAN WITH A CIRCLE MIND
BUT THAT BREAKS 2 LINES IN 2.
SO NOW I HAVE FOUR LINES THAT EAT UP MY TIME
THEY CAN'T TRAP MY MIND,
BUT THEY CATCH MY SPINE
WITH THIS CEMENT MATTRESS ASSIGNED
TO CELLBLOCK 9
DREAMING ABOUT MY QUEEN
BECAUSE SHE'S THE ONLY 1
THAT TOOK THIS 9 OF PASSION WITH A SMILE
I WISH I HAD 9 LIVES
IT FEELS LIKE I BEEN SHOT 9 TIMES
I'M NOT A 50 CENT NIGGA
IT TAKES A DOLLAR TO GET MY TIME
SAYS THE MAN WHOSE LIFE IS SPENT PAYING BILLS
AND POPPING BOTTLES WHILE HIS SOUL CRIES
I THINK TO SHINE THE LIGHT OF A CIRCLE MIND
TO SHOW THE CIRCLE SPINE OF A GENERATION
THAT DOESN'T HAVE TO LEARN WITH LINES
BUT THEY DROWN YOU WITH CRIME
AND MAKE YOU CRY A RIVER OF DREAMS
OF CIRCLES WANTING TO BE LINES
SO EVERY CHANCE I GET
I RAISE MY CIRCLE TO THE SKY
BUT THEN A SOUND REPLAYS
"BANG"
BULLSEYE!!!
ANOTHER CIRCLE BACK IN LINE.

SLAVES 2 THE TRUTH

PERCEPTION AND EXPECTATIONS
ARE SLAVES TO THE TRUTH.
THINGS ARE NOT WHAT
THEY SEEM.
ANYTHING CAN BE A DRUG
AS LONG AS THERE'S FEIN.
DO WE TRULY UNDERSTAND
THE CONCEPT OF BEING CLEAN?

SUN vs. MOON

I'VE SEEN MOTHERS GIVE THEIR SONS
ALL THE LOVE THEY NEVER HAD.
THEN DEPOSIT ALL THEIR PAIN & SORROWS
& INSECURITIES INTO THEIR DAUGHTERS.
GIVING THEIR LOVE TO SONS BECAUSE
THEY LOOK JUST LIKE THEIR FATHERS.
INCARCERATING THEIR DAUGHTERS
INTO THEIR DEEPEST PAIN,
DARK SKIES, AND RAIN.
DESPITE ALL OF THAT,
SHE STILL BECOMES A STAR
BUT JUST BECAUSE SHE SHINING DOESN'T MEAN
SHE DOESN'T HAVE SCARS.
HOW DO STARS AND SUNS
SHINE IN THE SAME SKY?
HOW DO MEN AND WOMEN
COEXIST WITHOUT LIVING A LIE?
DOES HAPPILY EVER AFTER ONLY LAST
WHEN WE BOTH WEAR A MASK?
BRINGING HOME THE BACON
TO A HOUSEWIFE IS A THING OF THE PAST.
HOW CAN HUMAN EXISTENCE
CONTINUE THIS WAY?
HAVE MEN AND WOMEN
EVER BEEN ON THE SAME PAGE?

VALLEY OF THE SHADOWS OF LIFE

WALKING IN THE DARKNESS,
LOOKING FOR A LIGHT TO TURN ON!
I WAS TRYING TO SURVIVE.
I DIDN'T KNOW MY DECISIONS WERE WRONG.
HOW LONG MUST I SING THIS SONG?
THEY CHANGED THE NAME,
BUT IT'S STILL THE SAME GAME.
THE STREETS PAINT THE PICTURE WHILE
THE GOVERNMENT BUILDS THE FRAME.
BUT WHO AM I TO COMPLAIN?
I ALWAYS HAD FOOD TO EAT AND
SHOES ON MY FEET.
DESPITE ALL THE DEFEATS,
WHEN I OPEN MY EYES
I STILL FEEL COMPLETE.
LIFE IS AN OPEN BOOK TEST
BUT YOU'LL NEVER KNOW.
IF YOU PASSED UNTIL YOU REST,
SO DON'T LEAVE ANYTHING ON YOUR CHEST.
JUST APPRECIATE THE TIME THAT YOU HAVE LEFT.
YOUR SOUL IS NOT GOING TO
ALWAYS BE IN YOUR FLESH.
SO SAY LESS!
AND OVERSTAND THESE WORDS.
IF YOU CAN STILL HEAR YOUR HEARTBEAT, THEN
YOU DON'T NEED TO HEAR ANY WORDS
TO WRITE YOUR OWN RHYMES.
I'M HERE TELLING THE STORIES OF MY BROS THAT RAN OUT OF
TIME.
YOUR MESSAGE DOESN'T
HAVE TO BE ON LINES &
IF YOU NEED HELP,
PERSPECTIVE WILL HELP.
READ BETWEEN THE LINES.
YOUR LIFE STORY IS

**THE BOOK THAT YOU NEED TO READ
I'M JUST HERE TO PLANT THE SEED.**

1 DAY

HOW CAN YOUR SUNRISE?
WHEN YOUR MOON NEVER SET!
I'M CHEATING YOUR PROCESS
BY DEFLECTING YOUR PAIN.

SO WHO AM I?
TO LISTEN TO YOU
WHEN YOU COMPLAIN
ABOUT THE SHEETS
TO THE BED
YOUR NIGHTMARES
ARE IN.

ARE WE KIN?
OR DO WE JUST
SIN WITH OUR BODY
LOOKING FOR A WIN?

IN A TELEPHONE BOOTH
LOOKING FOR THE SUIT
I CAME WITH.
CAPE FULL OF HOLES LEFT
FROM MY SOUL BECAUSE
BEING A SUPERMAN
ONLY RESULTS IN BEING
ALONE.
I CAN'T ABSORB YOUR MISERY.
I DON'T WEAR THAT NAME.
I'M JUST A PRODUCT OF THIS
GRACE. HOPEFULLY ONE DAY
I HAVE THE COURAGE TO SAY THIS
TO YOUR FACE.

SAY HI

I'M SCARED TO SAY HI
BECAUSE IT'S JUST A
COUNTDOWN UNTIL GOODBYE.
IF IT'S NOT UNTIL DEATH
DO US PART THEN
I'M GONNA END UP LEAVING
WITH A PEACE OF YOUR HEART.

CULTURE VULTURE

YOU WORK SO HARD
TO INFLUENCE
THE CULTURE UNTIL YOU
GET LOST IN THE SAUCE
AND NOW THE ONLY WAY
TO EAT IS TO BECOME A VULTURE?

THIS IS MY CITY

LOOKING AT THE SKYLINE, TRYING TO DRAW THE LINE
BETWEEN MY PAST AND NOT BEING LAST.
I SEE THE MIGRATION TO MY CITY
AND IT'S LOSING THE GRITTY.
I GUESS THE PLAN WAS TO BE
LIKE DIDDY AND NOT LIKE BIGGIE.
BE AROUND LONG ENOUGH TO SEE YOUR CROPS GROW.
SELLING CRACK WHEN Y'ALL SHOULD HAVE BEEN BUYING
BROWNSTONES.
NOW ALL I SEE IS CONSTRUCTION ON BROWNSTONES.
I WISH THEY GAVE MY MOMMA
SOME OF THOSE WHITE LOANS.
BUT THE REALITY IS THEY PUSHING US
OUT OF THE CITY.
SO EITHER WE START THE TAKEOVER OR WE JUST PARTY ON
THE BLOCK UNTIL THEY TAKE OVER.
I LOVE THIS CITY FOR THE PEOPLE, NOT THE CHECK
EVERYBODY IS ON A MISSION TO TAKE OVER.
UNTIL YOUR MANAGER TELLS YOU
THAT YOUR BREAK IS OVER.
SO BACK TO THE BEAT.
IT'S THE PEOPLE THAT CREATE
THE VIBE IN THESE STREETS.
STOP SAYING YOU WANT TO COME TO MY CITY,
WHERE I LAY MY HEAD ISN'T PRETTY.
I'M TIRED OF THESE VULTURES
DO WHITE PEOPLE HAVE A CULTURE?

HEARTBEATS

DON'T LOVE ME
ONLY TO
THE CONVENIENCE
OF YOUR HEART.
LOVE ME WHEN
THE BEAT STARTS.

Mary Jane

Just the two of us
Equals...
Lust & Trust.
But
luck is something I find
when I spend time thinking
of you in my mind.
The fraction of you that's divided in two
is the gateway to my pleasure!
I feel your water run
free as you sink into my weather.
Seasons, these are the reasons
that we're here.
THC is adopted by the earth.
Wind blows up skirts so
fire keeps the loud clouds
building castles in the air.
How can love appear
without Fear?
I guess these are the things
you say when you're high.
A love story
about your bond with Mary Jane.
How there's nothing that
can take her place.
I have to let you go to grow.
One day I know
I'm going to see you
while shopping at the store.

P.S.: I know you would be proud of me; I learned how to fly without being in the sky.

You & I

You worry about what
I understand,
Why?
You hurt from the pain.
I learned how to cry.
You're scared to live.
I want to earn
the day I die.

The Love Jones

Being an artist is like being
on a date with fate.
How long can your mind relate
to all the plates
under the earth that has no
founding date?
I call it a Mental Quake.
Every artist has been in
a room and felt alone.
But today, I realize that
I was just on my phone.
Enslaved to the poles that
strip the soul of a diamond
that never seen gold.
I'm in a room with everybody
that grew up on Lauryn,
but we still love Cole.
That's why smoking this
Jay, while climbing this hill,
can never get old.
Enlightenment is meant
for us to grow
Because we all know how
depression goes.
So the motto will always be
starve the ego &
feed your soul!
I finally understand what they meant
when they say The Love Jones!
It's when you finally understand

that the conversation
of love starts with a dial tone.
I've waited my whole life
to reach this milestone!
Too many days have washed away
riding somebody's else's wave
But I have a message
from my flesh to my soul.
The message is your here to stay!
Life gets crazy when you start to understand
why Kanye loves Kanye.
Let me explain:
You get into a zone that makes
you look forward to your mistakes
because learning how you deal with your
mistakes are what make you great.
I don't know how many
mistakes it takes to be great
but I know that I'm 7 mistakes
closer to my break.
I call it the language of the greats.
It's when you're so in touch with
faith that you feel like you can
learn how to fly in 1 day!
I stand here today
as a living testimony of faith
because I'm the best thing
that I have ever been.
With all of my sins!
Because I can finally relate
to the fabric that I call my skin.
I'm just a soul in a body

that was born to win.
Because God tagged me saying
YOU'RE IT.
We are all born to win.
Every day I get to do something
that nobody has ever done.
I get to be me
and you get to be you.
We all can change this world.
How about we see it thru.
Love is now and
has always been the answer.
The only way to spread the love
is by loving you.

Bleeding Pen

When you pick up this pen,
know that it is not a Game.
It's not an easy road to fame.
This ink spill my pain
and it keeps me sane.
Trying to stay between these lines even
when there's traffic in my lane.
It's crazy how fans expect
an artist to stay the same,
as if we forfeit the right
to graduate from our pain.
I can't write what I don't feel,
so I don't understand how these rappers
make music to JUST pay bills.
Y'all think I wrote these words?
These words wrote to me.
These letters have a habit of
exposing all of my insecurities.
I have ghostwriters
that tell me bars about their time in chains & behind bars
& how they miss looking at the North Star.
My words aren't my words.
My pain isn't my pain.
Everything that comes out of me
is from my ancestor's name.
We all got something to say, but being a wordsmith is
when you're
able to put your pride away.
Say what people need, not what they want.
You can write your truth

but be careful of the FoNt.

My Mental Sins

I like you.
That wasn't hard to say.
But if I write that to you,
I have to wait
30 minutes for you to hit me back
and say, "What do you like about me?"
I don't know?!
I like your nose
because it feeds your brain
enough oxygen to stay alive
so I can see your smile.
I like you now
and I don't know
if I'm going to like you tomorrow
because an Instagram model might steal
my dopamine for desire.
I'm not trying to be your Romeo
, and I don't need a Juliet.
But I'll be lying if I said I don't
want to make you sweat.
I want to admire the perspiration flowing down your
melanin while my soul
is beating on your maple skin.
I hope the Lord understands my mental sins.
I don't know you but
I think I want to.
Ask about your childhood.
and see if you played Pokémon
blue red and gold 2.
I want to feed you and

see where our history relates
and if we have enough in common
then maybe a 2nd date.
I'll let you know from now,
I'm always about 30 mins late.
So here's my number
text me if you want a date.

914-548-2195

Marriage OVER Weddings

Why are we so scared of love?!
Why do we compare getting
our heartbroken to taking drugs?
Running away from our pain is
insane because you travel thru a
lucid dream to avoid the rain
just to land back in the
same airport of your pain.
Have you ever ask yourself,
why am I feeling this way?
Is it because my angels
left me while all my demons stayed.
Or is it because now
I have to find another pill to take?
Was is it real love (Mary J)?
My heart feels like it just
went thru 500 days of summer
and winter's around the corner
with an icebox where my heart needs to be.
Was this about you, or was it about me?
How was it a sacrifice if
neither of us paid a fee?
I'm not scared to love you.
But are you afraid to love me?
There's a lot of
soulmates dying in the friend zone,
While you're looking for a temporary
mate that has an expiration date.
You get made when it spoils
after you keep them

---

a couple of weeks too late.
We love out of fear!
We love with our eyes and our ears!
But love is that party between
your flesh & your soul that kind of feeling
that keeps you warm in the cold.
And if it's real, it gets better while you get old.
Love doesn't need a Re-election vote;
it's so powerful that it doesn't need a coat.
It can last thru all the seasons.
You have to give it a reason.
So do you treat love as a drug?
Or do you treat love like a hug?
I'm tired of holding on
to your perception of love
while I drag my emotions thru the mud.
This isn't that kind of love!
I'm not going to reward bad behavior
with a shrug or a hug.
We have to fight for this.
So b4 we kiss, and you become my Mrs.
We have to build a foundation to grow because
if our love languages stay the same,
our lust will trump the pain until
our fountain of youth is drained.
Then we will look at each other to blame.
Do you just want a dress and a ring? Or
Do you want to hear Toni Tony Tone sing?
If all we have is time, then let's just.
Leave it in the past.
My only question left is,
Do we have what it takes to make this love last?

Beauty Is Her Curse

Beauty is her curse.
Did you ever think that?
She likes playing
2K over wearing a purse.
But she's the newest thing that
quenches your thirst.
So you do things to make her
feel like she's in 1st place
like she's worth a house and marriage.
If you really knew her, you would know that
she never dreamed of a horse and carriage.
She is throwing mace playing Call of Duty
and her online name was @nomakeupsavage!
She has been blocking dudes shot
since the 6th grad.
Everybody thinks it's a phase
but just because she's beautiful doesn't mean
she has to spend her whole life telling men
no, or wondering if it's love.
Her beauty is the plug to living. Wondering if
She's enough because
every man views her as his drug.
Why do we assume that our fantasies
don't have their own dreams?
Grown men are making young girls feel A way.
Now they think that beauty is the only
way that the world will see them,
instead of valuing what she has to say.
How beautiful women make you feel A way?
We treat them like they're on Pornhub

and we can press play.
Hopefully, she has a strong usher in her life.
to show her how to do it her way.
Not objectifying her until she scared away from being
who she wants to be.
Did you know in middle school
she used to draw anime?
Gohan was her favorite character,
but now you devise a plan
to chase after her with your
140 characters? When you see
her all you see is your next bae.
You prayed on her like a sin.
Watched her until she was old enough to win.
There was a line, and you crossed it.
If you care,
leave her alone
and let her grow
until she the woman that's
strong enough to say no.
Her beauty is a gift, not a curse.
Let her determine her worth.

Soul Strippers

I met a girl that didn't
have a soul.
I never felt a body that
was so cold.
I'm not going to lie,
the profession
she chose was bold.
She makes money
dancing on a pole.
Every time she made
her ass clap
I felt her self-esteem
hit all-time low.
I don't care if I looked like a captain
save a hoe but
I just wanted to take
her out of that hell hole.
I wonder who in her life lacked the time
to show her another way to grind
but that's a story for another time.
Daddy issues run deeper than a 9 to 5.
Ain't no lunch break
when your someone's fantasy.
Stripping for men who
can't see the Angel that you could be.
But you put in that overtime so
OT OT OT
(Drake's voice)
I pray that every night
you make it home

in one piece.
I met a stripper at the Marriott, room 319.
She didn't have a pole,
and her pimp was about 6'4
no Shade.
But there isn't any sunshine
where's she going.
I can't predict the future
her pimp could have had the Draco[3].
I OD feel like Drake thou
because the time that we have to be alive
is more than wearing Bape and
showing up to work late.
Well this is just the story
of a girl who lost her soul
that I meet in the hotel room in 404.
I know there are millions
of girls missing their souls
across different area codes
most of y'all don't care; you just say
"That's how the game goes."
I know I'm not the only one who cares.
But I ask myself every
day why was I even there.

---

[3] Draco is also slang for a gun.

Miseducation Of

I'm not saying
she's a gold digger,
but she spent
her whole life looking
for that glow.
Trying to fly like an angel
but her wings are broken.
Spent too much time in the dirt
and her flower didn't grow.
So her seeds are lost
in her soul,
so she falls in love with everything
that shines
but we all know that just because
it glitters doesn't mean it's gold.
She wasn't born a gold digger
she was down to earth
when she had
a hidden figure.
But these baby boys
keep feeding her
snickers
so she thicker
and got the mentality of a boss.
She is going to use
what she got
so she doesn't have to pay the cost.

She was taught
closed legs don't get fed,
so now she only talks
to men who drive a Porsche.

Her sister was miseducated
on the game, and
she's happy because she doesn't want
fake fame.
She got her own mind and
she uses her body
to dine and drink wine while looking
fine but she wants
to live a good life on her own dime.
She learned how to grind on her own time
she's a woman of goals
that loves her soul and
she sometimes cries at night,
and the Lord knows.
Sometimes she thinks
about dancing on a pole
but she knows she
can't grind on men that are so cold.

There's a thin line between
living for gold and
accomplishing your goals.
Both women love J Cole;
One sister is in VIP
with a man; she does not know.
and the other sister is in the top row.

They both had no role modelz
and chose different paths.
One's not better than the other,
just remember
good looks go fast.
Don't look back at your past
And see an empty glass that
was once half full.
Being true to the essence of your soul
will always be worth more than gold.

Women's Mind

Women's Mind
is meant to shine.
only she knows how to
be a moon,
Shine like a star
And can raise a son.
That's why my heart
beats for your love.
Even though you said
you hate to party
But?
I saw you on the gram twerking with
your tongue out in the club.
I'm not the 1 to judge
I just don't understand
how you want to be loved.
You were raised on Mary j
Jada and Nia Long
Idealize Lauren, Lil Kim and TLC
But now listen to
Nicki and Cardi B.
So I guess I HAVE to be
Dwayne Wayne mixed with
Dwayne Wade with a little bit of Tupac on top.
Take Care of your emotion like Drizzy Drake
& still, know how to make that Bed Rock!
I'm not going to lie, it's a lot.
Especially growing up in the race of babies.
That hate the ladies that make the babies
We never healed our women now

We can't be real with our women!
So we hurt bae
just to lay with the next girls
because she got a 100k
on the gram but when bae doesn't
come back to us; we like damn,
PAC told us this was going to happen!
Love is way more than
Henny bottles and magnums.
I guess you have to be lucky to find a bad 1
a woman who knows how to be a queen
& can be silly at random.
Know how to juju on that beat
electric slide
& still can do the bad one.
You can be any kind of
Queen you want
to be because
you don't need a king to
make you royalty

Why Should I Love You?

Why should I love you?
And not myself?

Those are the options
you put on the table
when you look
for validation
from someone else.

You value my pictures
more than my presents.

What's love got to do with
Flowers or chocolate
Or even good morning texts
But I follow the script because
I don't want to fall short
of what's expected.
Before our 1st date
you already programmed
yourself to think that I was the one.
That's the same feeling my mom felt when
she had a son.
"I'm going to have a man that
listens to my truth finally."
Do women love me?
Or what I represent?

Thoughts that I have after spending
98 cents on my emotional rent.

Mama Africa

Home is where the heart is.
Someone told me Africa
is where it all started.
But who's fault is it that
I'm wearing an American flag
to school to represent
my roots. It's crazy how they
played us for fools teaching
history that only dates back to their rule.
Not all Africans were slaves
Not all pilgrims were fake.
But you have to learn
how to read thru the maze.
Would Jesus be my lord and savior
if my ancestors
weren't enslaved?
Or would
I be standing on this stage explaining
the thoughts in my brain.
I'm not saying that Melanie is the best!
But when the sun shines its light on the world,
we absorb the light better than the rest.
That's why they try to keep
us away from our throne
Mama Africa
I miss you
I'm coming home.

The 25TH Hour

You prepared me for a world that
doesn't exist.
I walk the streets, and I see the
fear in people's eyes
because they know that everything
that they invested in is going to die.
Pensions could be worth a billion
but who cares if the dollar is
on a countdown to its demise.
Soon time isn't going to relate.
To the beat of these screens
Because reality lives in the mind.
I live in the future while
my parents hold on to the past
Nobody knows how long either one
is going to last
YouTube taught me more than class.
But living on screens allow
you to wear too many masks.
Where do I stand?!
Born in 1990 so I remember the vintage plan!
Get a degree than a job and some land.
But then the internet shocked the world.
Now girls want VVS, not pearls.
Who predicted this life?
Is life only the perception of
the expectation of the truth?
If we can't be perfect
then why is there
schools or rules or pools

with deep ends.
If I never met your soul.
When we die
how can we be friends?

Barcodes

Name your price
In life and
do it before
the Fame or the chains.
Name your price
when you still love the game
When you are dealing
with regular life pain.
How much does your loyalty cost?
Can your love be bought?
Are your insecurities
a thing of the past
or are you free of
fear because you have
Henny in your glass?
Are you still afraid to raise
your hand in class or
you can't focus because
the girl next to you is shaped
like an hourglass?
What's your price tag on Focus?
Do you lose it trying to
bite ever peach that
falls from a tree?
Or
Do you sit in the shade
scared to see the
sunrise tomorrow
thinking about the payment
due on the sadness

you left in your sorrow?
What makes you sad now?
At 6 you were
only sad when mom said you
couldn't play.
At 12 you were sad because
your dad was stuck in Jamaica.
At 14 you were sad when
the light-skinned girls
didn't want to call you bae.
At 21 the only sad thing
was my bank account
but I had those new Jays.
Now the only thing that
makes me sad is when
my friends pass away and
when little girls feel like
they're not pretty because
they have a dark face.
These barcodes
change every day.
I thought
I knew what
I wanted from love
Then God showed
me a new way.
So my price of Shame
became a part of the game because
I can't speak my truth
without telling you my pain.
In middle school,
they used to make

fun of my name,
now they say it's beautiful
so I guess the
price changed.
I wish they had a buy
one get one free coupon
for fame because there's
so much talent in the
streets, all of you just
don't know their names.
The price of my anger put me
in a different tax bracket of stress.
Society tells me every day that
I'm lucky because my soul
didn't escape my flesh.
My inventory has taken
a hit because
I let people steal from
my store without reporting it.
When I do my next Audit
I know,
I'll be missing about
10 pounds of faith
and a couple boxes of trust
two selves of lust
and a bottle of luck.
They stole my grind, but I had
Insurance on that,
so I'll be fine.
They made sure they didn't take
my insecurities or my broken dreams
or the fake gold chain my mom

bought because she
wanted me to be clean.
What's your price to be free?
I don't know
how much you need
But
I just got a loan
from God
to invest
in the business of ME!

Waiting to Create?

What artist waits to create?
You do!
That's why you wait to live the life
you've always wanted
knowing the history of fate!
We all have a date
that no matter
what we wear or
the color of our hair
it's going to take us out of here!
We all die! & sometimes that thought
makes me cry but
death is beautiful because it's
the common denominator to all of our lives.
My art is my message
a part of me dies every
time I sketch it.
You judge me for my words
because it gives you perspective
but I'm just trying 2 pass on the message.
You can hide behind
a race or how much money
you make, but you still have a date with fate!
So why wait to create?
Everybody is an artist: you have to find
the platform you want to paint.
Hurry up b4 it's too late.
A real artist doesn't wait to create

ACKNOWLEDGEMENTS

I LEARNED A GREAT DEAL ABOUT MYSELF DURING THE DIFFICULT PROCESS OF WRITING THIS BOOK. THE COMPLETION OF THIS WORK WOULD NOT HAVE BEEN POSSIBLE WITHOUT THE UNWAVERING SUPPORT OF MY FRIENDS AND FAMILY. THEY ARE THE TRUE DEFINITION OF COMMUNITY.

I'M ETERNALLY GRATEFUL TO MY MOTHER, PATRICIA APPLETON, WHO LOVES ME UNCONDITIONALLY. SHE TAUGHT ME LOVE, RESPECT, AND OTHER TOOLS THAT HAVE HELPED ME SUCCEED. I GENUINELY HAVE NO IDEA WHERE I'D BE IF NOT FOR HER SIGNIFICANT BELIEF AND SUPPORT OF MY DREAMS.

TO MY SISTER ALICIA WHO PLANTED THE SEEDS OF CREATIVITY AND KNOWLEDGE IN MY MIND AT AN EARLY AGE. YOU GAVE ME EVERYTHING I NEEDED MENTALLY AND EMOTIONALLY, EVEN WHEN I DIDN'T WANT IT. THE TOUGH LOVE AND DISCIPLINE WERE NECESSARY WHEN I WAS LOST AND TRYING TO FIND MY WAY. NO MATTER WHAT I DID YOUR LOVE WAS LIMITLESS. I KNOW I'M YOUR HEART, AND I DON'T TAKE THAT FOR GRANTED. I LOVE YOU FOR BEING A GREAT SISTER, GREAT MENTOR AND FRIEND.

TO MY FATHER, DONALD APPLETON, I THANK YOU FOR ALWAYS KEEPING ME GROUNDED AND SHOWING ME OUR CULTURE AND HISTORY. YOU ALWAYS GAVE ME THE SPACE TO BE MY OWN MAN AND FIND MY OWN WAY. I WAS MAD GROWING UP BECAUSE I WASN'T A JUNIOR, BUT YOU ALWAYS TOLD ME, "I WANT YOU TO BE YOUR OWN MAN. DON'T LIVE IN MY SHADOW."

TO MY BROTHER EDSON, I LOVE BRO. WE SPENT SO MUCH TIME TOGETHER GROWING UP, AND THOSE EXPERIENCES ARE PRICELESS. THANK YOU FOR BEING THERE AND PUSHING ME TO BE GREAT EVEN WHEN WE DIDN'T SEE EYE TO EYE.

ALTHOUGH THIS PERIOD OF MY LIFE WAS FILLED WITH MANY UPS AND DOWNS, MY TIME AT FOOTLOCKER WAS WORTH IT. MY TIME IN THE SNEAKER INDUSTRY TAUGHT ME SO MUCH ABOUT PEOPLE, BUSINESS, CUSTOMER SERVICE, AND PRODUCTION.